SUKKAH–DOODLE–DOO!

WHAT IS A SUKKAH?

A sukkah is a temporary booth, or shelter, where meals are enjoyed with family and friends. It is built and decorated each autumn for the seven-day festival of Sukkot. The Hebrew word *sukkah* means "booth." It is the singular form of the plural word *sukkot*, or "booths," which is also the name of the festival!

Sukkot's a treat—a time of thanks
For life, for food, for home.
A sukkah is a place of joy:
Hello! Come in! Shalom!

A Sukkah's Roof . . .

Its roof is made of things that grow:
Branches, twigs, bamboo.
It's not completely covered, though—
The sun and stars shine through!

Sukkot remembers:

- The Israelites' 40-year journey in the wilderness towards a new home and freedom in the Promised Land—a land of milk and honey.
- The temporary shelters—the *sukkot*—that they erected to dwell in along the way.

Sukkot also celebrates the fall harvest, which is why fruits and vegetables are often used as sukkah decorations.

sukkah: **sook**•uh; *sook* rhymes with *book*
sukkot and Sukkot: sue•**coat**
shalom: shah•**lohm**; hello

SUKKAH-DOODLE-DOO!

A Holiday to Crow About

Written by
MARGIE BLUMBERG

Illustrated by
TAMMIE LYON

Inspired by a story by
KAY KANTOR POMERANTZ

MB PUBLISHING

Autumn leaves are showy
Like my multicolored feathers.
Invitations have been mailed
For sukkah get-togethers.

The Mindel family's tickled pink:
Sukkot is drawing near.
There's lots to do—
Come join them!
It's a splendid time of year . . .

Fetch your things, Jimmy.
Fall breezes are blowing.

Shelley, I'm ready.
But where are
we going?

Out for adventure.
The wind's whistling, "Hey!
A sweet celebration
Is heading our way."

You know what that means?
It's twig-finding time!

Ooh, that's a *leafy* one—
Truly sublime.

You seem kind of tuckered.
I know what we'll do.
There's a log in our yard
That's just waiting for you!

What is that knocking?
Woodpeppers, Sis?

No, but good guess.
Follow me!
Look at this . . .

We're building a sukkah—
That's the loud fuss.
A bird's bringing twigs
For the roof—just like us!

For seven whole days,
We'll enjoy this big booth.
We'll eat, sing, and giggle—

I'll wiggle my tooth!

What's next? Decorations!
Time to make this place grand.
Ruffles can help—
He can give us a hand.

Letters are fancy
With glitter—*woo-hoo!*

Beautiful, *mazel tov* . . .

Sukkah-doodle-doo!

Raisins add sweetness.
Almonds add crunch.
Your kugel will shine
At our holiday lunch!

JOIN US!

It's much too soon for dreidels. The shofar has been blown.
But look—Sukkot is coming. It's time! Say yes by phone.
The date: October 20th. One-ish will be fine.
We just can't wait to see you—to chat and sing and dine!

Love,
THE MINDELS
Janet, Adam, Shelley, Jimmy,
and Ruffles

Schedule
· muffins
· soup
· glasses
· dishes

9:58

Janet
Cookies are a
Dream crumb true

A FEW DAYS LATER:

Soup in two minutes.

Matzoh balls—
Yum!

Make way for
glasses . . .

And plates—
Here I come!

MENU

Apples and Honey
Kasha Knishes
Muffins and Soup
Filo Dough Fishes
Sweet Noodle Kugel
Mandel Bread, Too
Fruit Salad, Kichel
And Rugelach—Whew!

Ta-da!

Table's set!

Look, Mom—surprise:
Ladybug place cards!

Aw, cuddle time, guys.

Company's coming—

Race to the door!

Oy, we've got TROUBLE . . .

ONE,
TWO,
THREE—
FOUR!

Follow me, Shelley,
Nana, Mom, Pop—

Worms to the rescue . . .

HOP,

HOP,

HOP,

HOP!

You need

your *own* sukkah.

And when I am through . . .

Invite some guests over . . .

Sukkah-doodle-doo!

Jimmy's our hero!
My brother thinks fast.
Hooray—time to shout:
   Chag sameach at last!

ONE HOUR LATER:

Shelley made kugel
And wrote a HIT song.
The melody's CATCHY.
Hint-hint—sing along . . .

Sing to the tune "Take Me Out to the Ball Game."

Let's go out to the sukkah—
It's spectacular there.
Nature's included with every meal.
~~You could say that it has real appeal.~~
But <u>toad</u>-ay, we had quite an ordeal!
Pull your chair right up to the table
And chat with family and friends.
Feel the sunshine,
Gaze at the stars—
Hope it never ends!

Today was really *hopping!*
Tomorrow, *our* place.

Your kugel was scrumptious . . .

Bring worms—
Just in case!

Shelley, my tooth!

It was never in doubt.

I started to nosh,
Then . . .

Gosh—

It fell out!

Your printing looks nice.
This letter sounds right.
I sure hope the tooth fairy
Reads it tonight.

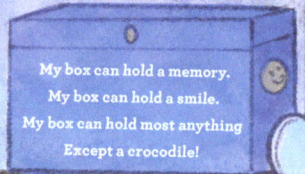

My box can hold a memory.
My box can hold a smile.
My box can hold most anything
Except a crocodile!

My
Fish

Dear Tooth Fairy,
This is my first lost tooth,
which I'd like to keep forever.
So if it's not against the
rules, when you leave the
gift (thank you!), please
don't take my tooth away.
Sincerely,
Jimmy

If *I* meet the fairy,
I'll tell her, OK?
Don't worry—I've got this.
I know what to say.

My box is oh-so stylish.
It holds my things in place.
And every time I open it,
A smile lights up my face!

My Uke

We'll always remember—it's hard to forget
Four toads, first lost tooth . . .

OUR BEST
SUKKOT YET!

That's the tale of this Sukkot,
A week I'll long remember.
It comes back every fall, you know—
October or September.

Next year, when it's time again
And the Mindels build anew,
They'll celebrate and sing our song . . .

Sukkah-Doodle-Doo!

SWEET WORDS

chag sameach (Hebrew) ~ happy holiday: a holiday greeting; *chag* means "holiday"; *sameach* means "happy" (**khag** sah•**may**•a<u>kh</u>).

kichel (Yiddish) ~ a sweet bowtie-shaped cookie (**ki<u>kh</u>**•uhl).

knish (Yiddish) ~ a ball of dough stuffed with seasoned mashed potatoes (or some other filling, such as cheese or fruit) and baked (kuh•**nish;** plural, knishes: kuh•**nish**•iz).

kugel (Yiddish) ~ a baked noodle or potato casserole (**kuh**•guhl).

mandel bread (English) ~ (from the Yiddish *mandelbrot*); literally, almond bread; a biscotti-like twice-baked cookie, but with a softer texture (**mahn**•duhl bread).

mazel tov (Hebrew) ~ congratulations (**mah**•zuhl tohv).

Mindel (English) ~ a Jewish surname, from the Yiddish feminine name *Mindl*, meaning "comfort" (**mihn**•duhl).

mitzvah (Hebrew) ~ a good deed (Sephardic Hebrew: meets•**vah;** English, Ashkenazic Hebrew: **mits**•vuh).

nosh (Yiddish) ~ snack *(nosh rhymes with gosh).*

oy (Yiddish) ~ an exclamation of dismay, grief, or exasperation *(oy rhymes with toy).*

rugelach (Yiddish) ~ literally, little twists; a small cookie made with a cream-cheese dough that is rolled around a filling (such as nuts, chocolate, or jam) and baked (**ruhg**•uh•luh<u>kh</u>).

shalom (Hebrew) ~ hello, goodbye, and peace (shah•**lohm**).

sukkah (Hebrew) ~ a sukkah is a temporary shelter, or booth, built for the seven-day holiday of Sukkot, also called the Feast of Booths (**sook**•uh; *sook* rhymes with *book*). Sukkot (sue•**coat**, in Sephardic Hebrew) recalls both the Israelites' journey from Egypt to the Promised Land—after having endured years of slavery—and the shelters they built in the wilderness. The festival also celebrates the fall harvest, when the last fruits of the fields and the orchards are gathered. The holiday falls on the 15th day of the Hebrew month of Tishrei under the full harvest moon. The English spelling of the Ashkenazic Hebrew and the Yiddish name of the festival is Sukkos (**sook**•kess; *sook* rhymes with *book*; *kess* rhymes with *cus* in *hocus-pocus*). In Yiddish, *sukkah* is pronounced **suh**•keh.

tzedakah (Hebrew) ~ charity (Sephardic Hebrew: tsuh•dah•**kah**; Ashkenazic Hebrew: tsuh•**daw**•kuh).

<u>kh</u> = the sound heard when you pronounce *ch* in J. S. *Bach*.

uhl = the sound heard when you pronounce the second syllable in the word *bagel*.

SHELLEY'S SCRUMPTIOUS NOODLE KUGEL

Serves 12.

KAY KANTOR POMERANTZ'S
FAMILY RECIPE

1/3 cup vegetable oil

4 eggs, beaten

1 16-oz package
egg noodles

1 tsp
vanilla extract

Ground cinnamon for dusting

Slivered almonds
for topping

1/2 cup sugar

1/2 cup raisins

1 cup
applesauce

2 Tbsp grated sweet onion

Optional additions: chopped
dates, apricots, or pecans

1. Preheat oven to 350°F.
2. Bring a large pot of lightly salted water to a boil. Stir in the noodles and return to a boil.
3. Cook the noodles uncovered, stirring occasionally until *al dente* (tender but firm)— about 5 minutes.
4. Drain in a colander and then pour the noodles into a large bowl.
5. Mix in the oil. Stir in the eggs, the remaining ingredients, and any optional additions.
6. Pour into a lightly oiled 9"x12" baking pan. Dust the batter with cinnamon and top with slivered almonds.
7. Cover with foil and bake for 30 minutes.
8. Remove the foil and bake for an additional 20-30 minutes until golden brown.

SARAH MINDEL'S MANDEL BREAD

Makes 42 cookies.

MARGIE BLUMBERG'S FAMILY RECIPE

2¾ cups all-purpose flour

1 cup semisweet chocolate chips

⅛ tsp salt

1 cup sugar

3 large eggs

1 tsp almond extract

1 tsp vanilla extract

1 cup canola oil

Cinnamon sugar

2½ tsp baking powder

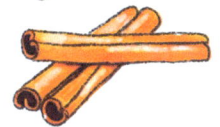

½ tsp ground cinnamon

1. Beat the sugar and oil together for two minutes with an electric mixer at medium speed.
2. Beat in one ingredient at a time (in this order): 3 eggs (also one at a time), vanilla extract, almond extract, and cinnamon. Set aside.
3. Sift together the flour, baking powder, and salt.
4. Add the flour mixture to the sugar/egg mixture and mix on a low speed until well combined. Fold in the chocolate chips by hand.
5. Cover the dough-filled bowl with aluminum foil and place on a shelf in the freezer for one hour.
6. Preheat oven to 350°F.
7. Prepare the cookie sheet with a nonstick spray.
8. Mold the dough into three rectangular logs (about 11" long x 2.75" wide) on the cookie sheet.
9. Sprinkle the top of each log with cinnamon.
10. Bake on the middle rack for 20 minutes.
11. Prepare the cinnamon sugar. (1:5 ratio: 1 Tbsp + 1 tsp cinnamon and 6.5 Tbsp sugar.)
12. Remove the cookies from the oven and close the oven door. Cut each log (while hot on the cookie sheet) diagonally into 14 slices and then flip the slices onto their sides.
13. Keeping the door closed, turn off the oven. Sprinkle the slices with cinnamon sugar and then immediately return the cookies to the turned-off oven for an additional 20 minutes.
14. Transfer the cookies to wire racks for cooling.
15. When the cookies have reached room temperature, either freeze them or pack them in an airtight container and store at room temperature for up to one week.

Sukkah-Doodle-Doo!

Sing to Chorus of "Give My Regards to Broadway"*

Original Lyrics by Geo. M. Cohan
New Lyrics by Margie Blumberg

Music by Geo. M. Cohan

♩=120

Suk-kahs are fine and dan - dy— just steps a-way from home sweet home.

Tell all your friends that they are wel-come to come in— sha - lom, sha - lom!

Who first put up a suk - kah? The Is-rael-ites, of course— that's who.

Build to re - mem-ber ev - 'ry year and shout out suk - kah - doo-dle - doo!

Original Lyrics to the Chorus
Give my regards to Broadway • Remember me to Herald Square •
Tell all the gang at Forty-Second Street that I will soon be there •
Whisper of how I'm yearning to mingle with the old-time throng •
Give my regards to old Broadway and tell them I'll be there e'er long.

*"Give My Regards to Broadway" ©1904 F. A. Mills • 48 West 29th St., New York
From the play *Little Johnny Jones* and featured in the 1942 film
about Cohan's life, *Yankee Doodle Dandy*.
New Lyrics by Margie Blumberg ©2022 MB Publishing, LLC.

Let's Go Out to the Sukkah!

Play and sing to the tune of "Take Me Out to the Ball Game"*

Original Lyrics by Jack Norworth
New Lyrics by Margie Blumberg

Music by Albert Von Tilzer

♩=170

Visit MB Publishing to hear the song: https://mbpublishing.com/sukkah-doodle-doo

Let's go out to the suk - kah— it's spec - tac - u - lar there.
Na - ture's in - clu - ded with ev - 'ry meal. You could say that it
has real ap - peal.** Pull your chair right up to the ta - ble and
chat with fam - 'ly and friends. Feel the sun - shine,
gaze at the stars— hope it nev - er ends!

**Sing "You could say that it has real appeal," or sing Shelley's new lyrics: "But toad-ay, we had quite an ordeal!"

Original Lyrics to "Take Me Out to the Ball Game"

Take me out to the ball game • Take me out with the crowd •
Buy me some peanuts and Cracker Jack • I don't care if I never get back •
Let me root, root, root for the home team • If they don't win, it's a shame •
For it's one, two, three strikes, you're out, at the old ball game.

With oodles of love for Jim, my constant shelter in all kinds of weather.
And for my great-grandmother Sarah Mindl: with a tender heart, she
gave love and comfort to her family, and as treasurer of the Hebrew
Ladies Sabbath Free Loan and Charity Society, she performed the
mitzvah of *tzedakah* in her adopted hometown of Baltimore, Maryland.

—MB

For my family and all of the happy holiday memories we have shared together.

Love,

—TL

MORE MB BOOKS

Avram's Gift • Breezy Bunnies • Sunny Bunnies • A Gefilte Fishy Tale
Paris Hop! • Rome Romp! • A Home for Hope!
Bunny Romero's White House Adventure: The Whole Megillah!
No Naptime for Janie! A Hanukkah Tale
The Secret at Haney Field: A Baseball Mystery
Jake McGreevy Novels: Celtic Run • Chicago Bound • Paris Secrets
Escape in Time • Tutti's Promise • By Light of Hidden Candles
The Scoop on Good Grammar

FUTURE BOOKS

Busy Bunnies • Snowy Bunnies • Pisa Loves Bella

Sukkah-Doodle-Doo! A Holiday to Crow About

Revised Edition: November 2023

Text copyright © 2022 by Margie Blumberg

New lyrics by Margie Blumberg, © 2022 MB Publishing, LLC

Illustrations copyright © 2022 by Tammie Lyon

Book design: PageWave Graphics Inc.

All rights reserved.

First published in the United States by MB Publishing, LLC.

https://mbpublishing.com

Summary: Surprises are in store for a Jewish family celebrating the joyous holiday of Sukkot.

Photo credits: gradient autumn background © istockphoto.com/Anna Bliokh; leaf © istockphoto.com/belander

Library of Congress Control Number: 2023948947

Blumberg, Margie

Sukkah-Doodle-Doo! A Holiday to Crow About by Margie Blumberg; illustrations by Tammie Lyon

Paperback ISBN: 978-0-9624166-5-1

Hardcover ISBN: 978-0-9994463-6-2

About the Author

Margie Blumberg writes and publishes books for all ages, from toddlers to adults. Her own books include *Avram's Gift, No Naptime for Janie: A Hanukkah Tale, Bunny Romero's White House Adventure: The Whole Megillah!, Sunny Bunnies,* and *The Scoop on Good Grammar.* MB Publishing's other titles include *A Gefilte Fishy Tale,* written by Allison and Wayne Marks and illustrated by Renée Andriani; *Tutti's Promise* by K. Heidi Fishman; and *Paris Secrets: A Jake McGreevy Novel* (Book 3 of 3) by Sean Vogel. Margie lives in Bethesda, Maryland, with her partner, Jim Catler, who enjoys every opportunity to serve as chief taste-tester for the delicious recipes that are included in their Jewish holiday picture books. Visit mbpublishing.com to learn more.

About the Illustrator

Tammie Lyon's love of illustrating began at a very young age while drawing at the kitchen table with her dad. She recalls sitting for hours drawing things around the house and later presenting her art as gifts to her mother. After graduating with a bachelor's in fine arts from Columbus College of Art and Design, she worked as a staff illustrator for a major greeting card company and rose to become a director of the juvenile product line. As a freelance artist, Tammie has illustrated numerous books, including her own children's book, *Olive and Snowflake* (Marshall Cavendish), and has also created the art for posters, magazines, CDs, games, and clothing. Tammie lives in Cincinnati, Ohio, with her husband, Lee. Her two dogs, Amos and Artie, love spending the day with her in her studio. Visit her online at TammieLyon.com.

Kay Kantor Pomerantz, the mother of four—Joey, Ari, Cantor Alisa Pomerantz-Boro, and Cantor Raquel Pomerantz Gershon—and grandmother of nine, is the author of three cookbooks, including *Come for Cholent: The Jewish Stew Cookbook.* She also enjoyed a distinguished career in education, serving as Executive Director of the Jewish Education Council in Seattle, Washington, and as Assistant Director of the Department of Education of the United Synagogue of America. Kay and her husband, Rabbi Moshe Pomerantz, reside in New York.